velvet goodbyes

emily curtis

emily curtis

ISBN: 0692151427
ISBN-13: 978-0692151426

velvet goodbyes

We write poems
for our lovers,
we write poems for our culture,
for our people,
and for those
on their way to the heavens,
we write for the inconsistencies of life,
for the brave men and women who fight for us,
and for the cowards who do just the opposite,
we write for the living who struggle,
the ones who are plagued with disease,
we write for our ancestors,
and their ancestors,
and so on,

we write for the fear of not being able to write anymore.

-for my fellow poets

emily curtis

I.

emily curtis

These truths have been
resting on my lips
for years
& years
& years
but I just can't seem
to let them go.

-cat got my tongue

velvet goodbyes

I've found Independence
is the only one
I can rely on anymore.

She is kind to me because
she does not care
what they think.

She loves me because
she has no one
else to love.

She trusts me because
she knows I will
never break her heart.

emily curtis

I've been searching for
those silver linings
everyone is always
talking about, but
it's been hard...

Those damn clouds are just too gray.

She tells me, "don't judge a book
by its cover," yet she
spends 40 minutes each
morning doing her
makeup so that people
she barely knows will
think more of her.

-tell me how this makes sense

Take me back

I miss the days
when bare faces
were common,
and judgment
was still in the womb.

When clothes
were just something
we wore so that
we wouldn't be cold,
not something we
would be judged for.

When un-plucked eyebrows
weren't criminal,
and having outdated
Nike sneakers
was acceptable.

Where did this idea of fragility come into play
when speaking of women?

Haven't you ever witnessed a man
in the midst of a heartbreak?

You've got me feeling
blue
&
gray
&
all the other colors of sadness
&
despair
&
loneliness
that I've forgotten to mention.

-and I wish you'd stop doing this to me

velvet goodbyes

She carries his weight around with her
because he is not strong enough
to hold it
on his own.

"I don't mind," she tells me one day
when I asked her why she does it.

"He'd do the same for me," she says,

frowning.

Isn't it ironic?
You text them all day
but yet you are
still missing something.

You are still alone.

-human contact

velvet goodbyes

This is why you
will never know
the comfort of
having a friend
who doesn't keep
a secret stash
of knives
or
cross her fingers
behind her back.

-because you do the exact same

Define "Obsession"

"I wonder how many calories this has?"

"Can I just have a side salad please?"

"Does this dress make me look fat?"

"Does diet soda mean that there's less sugar?"

"It's almost swim suit season. I need to fit into my bikini…"

"Does this herbal tea help with weight loss?"

"No pizza for me today. I'm doing a cleanse."

velvet goodbyes

She forced it down
her throat and
prayed it'd make
her look
like
them.

Sadness

She comes and goes
like the clouds
and she'll cover
up all the lightness
in your life
just because she can.

velvet goodbyes

The last time I saw you my stomach went fuzzy as if it lost radio connection. You hugged me. Screw you for doing that. You knew I had no control over the way my heart chose to ignore your inconsistencies, the way my brain ignored the way you ignored me, and the last time I saw you my hands were shaking and you saw that.

Some part of you deep down knew that we should have been together longer, that you missed your chance for something good, something real.

And some part of me deep down knew that it could never be.

I painted my bedroom
walls with prayers,
plastered my hope
on every fake laugh
and smile I gave you
but you never noticed,
or maybe you did
and never cared.

But God I wish you had.

velvet goodbyes

It's been years now
and yet
I can't convince my
stupid
rotten
careless
brain
that I've moved on.

My heart races with
the cars on the highway
when I hear your name,
my face turns velvet red
when I see your face,
those eyes,
that smile.

-this is not a love poem

I am the sum of

loving too deeply
+
trusting too sparsely.

velvet goodbyes

I used to think my biggest weakness
was that I never had any hope.

Now, I fear, my biggest weakness
was that I had too much.

You say,
"I think I respected your boundaries, didn't I?"
as if I should be rewarding you
for your common decency.

How can you think
that you have done
me a favor by
meeting my expectations?

velvet goodbyes

I've been hoarding the memories
of stolen kisses
and unspoken words,
of the way you moved across a room,
and of they way you laughed unapologetically,
of our last words,
and our last goodbyes.

-they're all I have left

Loneliness

It bleeds though her fingers
onto everything she touches,
it seeps from her frown lines,
and reaches for a heartbeat
—any heartbeat—
shy, but desperate.

velvet goodbyes

Friendship doesn't come
around my house anymore.
I think she might be mad at me.
Maybe she likes the way my
tears bleach my pillow case,
the way my room hasn't
felt the footsteps of another human
being in so long, so so long, and
even then, when there were footsteps,
they weren't destined to stay.

emily curtis

I've been frantically trying
to combine the right words
to describe the unendurable pain
of being

                    alone.

Cowardice

All
we
do
is
run,

away from
our feelings,

to
hide
from
the
truth.

emily curtis

For so long I have just watched
as Opportunity walks by
because I have been too afraid
to stop him and
shake his hand.

velvet goodbyes

Your timidness is a disease
and it has spread to me.

How are we to coexist
when we have barely
enough confidence to
say hello?

I should probably
go to bed now,
my eyes are heavy,
my soul is tired.

But here I am, again,
writing about you.
And about how
I am waiting for you.

And about
how you just never
seem to come.

velvet goodbyes

There are words on my shelves
that I have yet to devour,
and I hate that they sit there
begging me to pick them up, taunting me
while I carry on with my life,
pretending to be busy.

emily curtis

I found a fault in your voice,
I found that stench was all of your lies,
you mask it well, though, with all
that gum chewing and sweet-talking.

-but you didn't fool me

velvet goodbyes

And you wonder why
they always leave you.

And you wonder why
your heart always aches
after they tell you
all these bitter truths.

The ones you often hear
 but never listen to.

-still you never change

emily curtis

The ending

And I forgot to tell you how
I knew it would end. I always knew.
But I approached 'us' how one would
approach a vacation. It makes you feel
all excited at the beginning, new places,
new people, and it's fun for a little while,
but then you go home and
realize you have
more to do in life
than just this.

velvet goodbyes

Though you left me
slowly,
bitterly,
like you knew you would all along,
I do not wish you
anything but happiness.

Someone like you
needs it more
than I do.

You don't realize how
hard it is to reach you.
Your layers are

so

      damn

            thick

What makes you
feel as though
you need to
protect yourself
from human beings
who are
just like you?

What threat do they pose?

velvet goodbyes

When I pray I spend
20 minutes on your
name alone because
I know just how much
you need it.

-it is up to you to decide if this is sarcasm or not

emily curtis

You could damn near kill me
and yet, if you apologized after,
I would probably forgive you.
This is a habit
I need
                to
                        let
                                go.

velvet goodbyes

Your lies

were a kaleidoscope of colors,
an optical illusion of
short words and fake apologies,
twisting and
spinning and
hypnotizing,
a mirror of nothings
distracting me from reality,

from the truth.

emily curtis

We form habits,
ones that we

repeat

repeat

repeat

every day of our
dreadfully boring lives,
and we never
realize that
by repeating
we are not
actually living,

just surviving.

velvet goodbyes

Sometimes I let myself think about angels
and wonder if they are any different from ghosts.

Today I looked through an old photo album

I will never be 5 again. I will never again
want to play with dolls, or know what it
feels like to be friends with a boy without
someone assuming I am dating him. I will
never again feel the magic that is believing
in Santa Clause, or get excited when the
Easter Bunny leaves eggs for me to discover.
I will never again be ignorant of the damage I
do to our ecosystem each time I throw away
a piece of plastic, or of what it means when a girl
says, "me too." I will never again know that feeling
of invincibility, never again feel carefree when exiting
my house without any makeup—not even concealer
to hide the tiredness. I will never again know the
satisfaction of going to bed at 7 P.M.
And I will never again
be able to solve a problem
and feel better
just by simply
hugging
my mom.

We used to wish to be grown-ups

Only God knows the moment in which
my childhood perished. It was a slow
death, no one saw it coming, and
no one could stop it, not even my
parents, who prayed it would stay.
I wish I could go back to that moment
and prolong it. Find a way to slow down
the time. We used to wish to be grown-ups.

Only God knows why.

Our roots
to this earth
run deeper
than the trees'.

Think of how crazy that is.

-and we are tearing it apart

"Walk among my body,"
She says,
"drink my blood,
use it all how you wish."

And we did. Maybe too much.

I hope she doesn't regret her offer.

-Mother Earth

Memory

I know one day He will
leave me. It's inevitable,
I know this. It won't
be something I'll be aware of.
I'll be talking one day,
telling a story,
and suddenly
He will slip away from me.

"But what happens when we run out of time?"

-what an excellent question

Proof

There is an old-fashioned heater to my left,
it has sat for years, restless against that wall.
Above me the ceiling has, at late, been
revealing her weakest points,
cracks that have been faded out
with paint and cover-ups,
but like a woman's makeup at the end of the day,
they cannot fully conceal the tiredness and the lines,
and the hardwood floors haven't seen a stain in years,
drops of paint have hardened like raindrops that never dry,
and the window has been letting
the cold breeze seep through,
he has been careless, forgetting to close tightly,
and I used to be the owner of such travesties,
but now, I fear, I am blending in among them,
fading into the small world I live in until
there is nothing left of me but that room,
the only proof
that I once existed.

velvet goodbyes

That
dull
ache
for more,
more than
whatever this is,
it sits,
sulking,
in the depths of
my heart.

White–tipped toenails,
low arched feet
and thin ankles,
a curve to her calves,
and knees
connected to thick tree trunks,
powerful and defined,
compensating for her weak hips,
a torso so short—I bet you've
never seen a girl whose lowest
rib touches the top of her hip bone
when she bends—a spine curved
in both a natural and an unnatural way
and shoulders wide—defined during swim season—
a chest flat like a pancake, arms
forceful and freckled—on her right
the freckles outline the great dipper—
a scar on her pinky finger from
one too many seconds lingering shut
in a truck door, a thin neck, lips red,
teeth finally settled after years of
being ordered around by metal,
a nose, long, two eyes she has yet to decide
the color on—they always look different to her—
thick, wild, caramel hair that stretches down
her spine past her waist, ever growing towards
the ground, hair that is always in the way but
what she considers to be her best beauty,
a reason she will never cut it, and
out of all this, she still finds it
hard to look in the mirror without
feeling she's lost.

Sally Jenkins

called me a slut one day
in gym class.
She stared at me
as one would a
city rat
and let that
one syllable
spill from her lips
as if she were speaking of
the color of one's hair,
a truth so true no one could deny it.
The corners of her lips rose
into a sly smile and
when my reaction pleased her,
she spun on her heals and laughed,
sounding like the
Wicked Witch of the West.

Sally Jenkins works
at a gas station now.

You watch history
repeat itself

time

&

time

&

time again

but you convince yourself
each time that it won't.

velvet goodbyes

If I had a dollar
for every time
I've been told
to "marry rich"
I'd be richer
than the man
I've been told to marry.

You have the complex of a Greek God,
the confidence of Kanye West,
the compassion of a killer whale,
the beauty of a hyena,
and the jealousy of ex-girlfriend.

-you are not genuine

velvet goodbyes

I'm your "go to"
when your "go to"
is busy.

Anger is feeling alone.
Anger is tears.
She bangs on your chest
until water swells in your eyes,
Anger is the sun when it doesn't rise,
Anger is thunder.
Not lightning,
thunder.
Anger is darkness,
Anger is fear,
fear of something that is not there,
Anger will sweet-talk you into hatred,
Anger likes it when you're
begging at her feet for revenge,
Her food is your screams,
Her water is the sweat and tears that stain
your pillow at night
while you're tossing and turning
and you, your body,
that is her home.

velvet goodbyes

Broken clocks
hang from the walls
of our twisted house,
the kitchen faucet leaks,
the floors are cement and stained,
broken shards of glass
lay below empty windows as if
you once forgot a key and
had to smash them to break in,
the doors have no locks now,
they open and close on their own,
I shatter light bulbs below my feet
as I walk along these warped halls,
you said you built it all for me
and now,

I believe you.

I believe you.

Not even a heartbeat

Your words,
they storm through the room,
the chaos and rage
destroys the furniture,
tears at the curtains,
rips the couch in two,
but more importantly,
your wrath finds its way
into my heart, blustering
all through it until
there is
nothing
left.

velvet goodbyes

Chaos offered her home to me
and I accepted because
Calm had left me
for dead.

emily curtis

I was that trophy
you wanted
so badly
when you were 8 years old,

you know,
the one you
worked so hard for,

the one that now
sits in the back
of your closet
along with your
other forgotten toys.

velvet goodbyes

I have been played by you
so many times
that I have lost track,
and I have stopped counting
the "I'm sorrys"
every time you
let me down
yet
I forgive
&
I forget
so
damn
easily.

And out of it all
I remember your hands.

I'm not going to say they were
soft like the rain because they weren't.
They were rough and ungracious
and full of recklessness.
It was unlike me
to hold such skin on bones,
so dangerous and full of secrets.

But for some reason
I convinced myself
that they would be
the only ones
I would care to feel.
That they would be enough

for a while.

velvet goodbyes

Acceptance has been telling
me to let you go but
Hope won't let me.
Hope says you might
come back.

"He has hurt you a thousand times," Acceptance says to
her, defending me, "what makes you think he will change?"

"He has a heart in there somewhere," Hope shoots back.

This conversation goes on
for hours
&
hours
and neither
can ever
gain any ground.

-I never know whom to believe

Summer
was replaced
by a
winter
so brutal
that the
butterflies you gave me,

they went away.

When you left me broken I felt

Sad when it poured,
when it was sunny,
sad after every sharpened pencil snapped,
sad in the shower when I sang,
sad when I laughed at jokes that weren't funny,
sad when your sweatshirt landed in the trash bin,
sad in the mornings, evenings,
even when the Patriots played,
sad when the flames died down
and all that remained were the ashes,
sad when the leaves turned red,
and orange, and yellow, then brown,
sad when the snow came and
I no longer wanted to build a snowman,
sad even after my favorite songs
blared through the tired speakers of my car,
sad when I thought of you,
sad when I thought of her,
sad when you came back,
sad when I said no.

Once upon a time
a girl grew up
accepting her face
and natural beauty
for what it was
and then a boy,
worried about his own insecurities,
said to this little girl, pointing at her face,
"You have a unibrow!"
so she plucked
and she picked
until those hairs were gone,
but they always grew back.

A year later she saw a magazine
with a woman
thin
tall
blonde
posing for the front page,
she looked down at her own
pale pudgy body and
questioned it for the first time.

A few more years later
and an older friend of
this girl said to her,
"Without makeup I'd look like a zombie,"
and the girl glanced at her reflection
and sighed, seeing the resemblance of
her own skin to that of a
dead rotting fictional monster.

This story, as you may assume,
has no ending.

18
and I am
still
trying to figure out
who I am
while
the people around me
seem to already
know.

The mean reds

Today hasn't been a
good day.
Neither was yesterday,
and, come to think of it,
neither was the day before.
It is as if the sky has
cast a gloomy mood
over my soul and
it has yet to clear up,
the sun has yet to rise,
and the clouds have
yet to clear. This happens
every so often, you know,
my heart is just too easily
broken. It is true.
It doesn't take much for
that feeling of despair
to wash over my body,
but there is usually a cause.
This time, though, I am
not positive what it is.
I thought it was you,
you who was making me
feel as though I was
drowning helplessly
while standing completely still.
But now, I feel, it is
something much more
than that. It is a fear
much stronger than this
and I just can't put
any words to it.

II.

It will break you even more
if you try to fight it.

-healing

velvet goodbyes

I'm tired of being
ruthlessly polite
&
quietly defenseless.

emily curtis

I want to yell at you sometimes,
shout all the truths I've been burying
so that you wouldn't see how much I cared,

maybe then you would hear me
and see just how much
my heart has been aching for
your heart.

Reality

We're all just out here
wishing for security
and hoping for love.

I need to stop searching for inspiration
in the tender eyes of boys who are
too afraid to love me.

velvet goodbyes

I'm waiting for
the silence between us
to be comfortable.

Midnight thoughts

It is silent here.
Everyone's heads
are pressed into
their pillows,
all but one.

A small lamp is all I have
to dimly light
my oasis.

velvet goodbyes

I tell myself to cherish the cold nights,
because it's far colder
where I could have been,
down where everything rots
down where everything is lost
down with my great-grandparents
and great-great-grandparents
and so on
and so on

    and

            so

                    on

and this is now"

One day
I will look back
at this time and
wonder why
I couldn't see
how simple things are.

And I know I will say to myself,
"well, that was then,

velvet goodbyes

Why bother with
mouth-breathers and morons
just for a set of lips to kiss
under the starlight?

Waiting patiently
knowing that
new beginnings are
right around the corner.

-an impossible task

velvet goodbyes

I have stopped trying to
become the type of girl
I think you want because
you were never the type
of guy that would even notice.

-and besides, my version of me is better

March 8th

You raise babies,
you run households,
but you also raise the stakes,
change the game,
you are inventors,
bosses,
co-workers,
writers,
trend-starters,
musicians,
lawyers,
painters,
doctors,
athletes,
and any other thing you can think of
that we have been told we can't be.
That is what you are.

I can't wait to see
where you will
all go
from here.

velvet goodbyes

Go ahead,
try to break us,
stop us
from
          progressing
                              forward
but look how far
we've come,
doesn't that
say something?

-you can try, but you will not succeed

What we have been told "we" are

We are bossy
we are moody
we are emotional
we are petite
we are dainty
we are delicate, fragile
we like pink
we like flowers
but not when they die
we like things clean
we like romance
we wear dresses
and we share secrets
while we take group trips
to the bathroom
we complain often
we crave attention
and we never are satisfied with what we have.

What we are

We are not bossy
we are assertive
we are not moody
we just have feelings
we are not emotional
we have emotions
we are not dainty
and we are definitely not fragile
we are strong and hard to break
even some of the toughest men can't crack us
we are not just the color pink
we do not all love flowers
we can get messy
and we are independent
we wear ripped jeans
and are great at hiding our secrets
we do not need your attention for us to feel worthy, and
we are perfectly satisfied with our lives
even when you're not in them.

Paint the skyscrapers pink
and then all the other colors with it
we like them all,
we are all of them
and none of them
all at the same time,
we are colorful,
not a color
not one
single
color.

-pink

And it is Her alone
who is pushing,
forcing me,
to write this
very poem at a time when
I feel as though I have
nothing new to say.

-Determination

Together we

can convince men that
our bodies are not a
piece of property for
them to own,

can show our strength
through truths finally
spoken out loud,

can say goodbye
to stereotypes,

can eliminate the
gap, shatter that
thick glass ceiling,

can prove our worth
by showing that we
have been worthy
all along.

velvet goodbyes

She has been around for
almost 300 million years,
did you know that? She
was one of the first of
her kind to fly, and yet,
when she passes by your
window in the summer
I bet you think nothing
of her. She is just another
distraction to you.

-The Dragonfly

I do not
need you
to not
feel
alone.

My own
company
is just
fine.

-affirmations

Because we are getting stronger, you know,
there are more of us,
and we are smarter than you think,
our rights are growing,
and our hearts are too,
and our determination,
and our power,
and we,

we are changing things.

-the future is female

emily curtis

Progress is accepting
that the past has happened
and using it to your advantage
to do better
the
next
time.

-she is kind, and she is waiting

New Year's Resolutions:

1) Stop pretending that everything's fine all the time.
2) Do something unpredictable for once.
3) Don't care what they think.
4) Stop hiding behind your comfort zones.
5) Confront those feelings.
6) Forget him.
7) Find your own inspiration. You don't need a boy for that.

She works hard
to get where she wants to go
and she doesn't let
anyone enter her life
who doesn't deserve to be there.
She knows what her priorities are
and she doesn't stray
far from them.

She lives for her own happiness,
not for yours.

velvet goodbyes

I am the cracks in the pavement,
the splinters in the hardwood,
I am the ripple in a calm water,
the mud on a leather boot,
I am the shattered glass after
yelling in the kitchen, the ice
that freezes the pipes,
I am the epitome of a long,
hard day.

-this is my warning sign

emily curtis

Cute.

That's what you call me?
Please.
Don't patronize me.

At times I can be far from
"cute."

-you'll regret saying that

velvet goodbyes

I know they think it's a bad thing,
to be alone. They assume if you
sit by yourself, or go to prom without
a date, it is because no one wants you.
It is because you have tried to find
someone and have failed. It is because
you can't get a guy. It is a bad thing.

But no. They have never assumed
that sometimes you actually want to be alone.
That you don't always need another heartbeat
to make you feel whole. That your
independence is often key to your personality.
Something you pride yourself on. Because,
who would pride themselves on being alone?
Who would chose that life?

-I would

Low battery

11 P.M. coffee,
long-lived yawns between sips,
books scattered on beds,
minds brimming with information
that will be forgotten within hours,
"where on earth did all the time go?"
we ask ourselves
as another day slips
behind our eyelids
when we close them
to (hopefully) sleep.

The metronome

And as any good musician should,
I abide by the tempo, following
the rules, playing all the right notes,
but all the while I am longing for
a change in pace,
a different melody,
a solo.

emily curtis

I've always loved
how birds are
in sync when they fly,
"like a big wave," my dad would say,
and I would nod
in agreement
staring at them
in awe.

velvet goodbyes

The snow lands
quietly on the branches
of old trees like dust,
the whiteness is
like a fresh start and
each time it falls
I can't help but
romanticize it like one
would in a movie,
the pines are magnificent
when topped with that
pearly white sugar and
I admire it all, except
for when the rain then
washes it away and
the bugs and little
creatures emerge
from hiding and the
mud sticks to my boots
like molasses.

I've been saving up,
collecting couch change,
stealing sidewalk pennies,
for a voice
that will
freely speak
what it wants
for once.

To all the girls who think the abuse is acceptable
because he is your "soulmate,"

no.
There are
hundreds
thousands
millions
of men
who know
the difference
between
yes & no
you just
need
to wait
for them.

And right now
I'm just wishing
there was a
better word
to describe you
than "fake."

-because honey, you deserve a ~~better~~ worse word

velvet goodbyes

I pretend to know about
lots of things, whether it be
books,
or authors,
or music,
or art,
or so on
and so on,
but I will never try to
pretend as though I have
wrapped my brain around
such a confusing idea
as "men."

"Hush now," Clarity says
to me, soothingly,
"I will come to you soon.
Be patient, my love."

velvet goodbyes

Everyday moments and things

A hand gently swaying out a rusty
car window driving down the highway,
sore ribs from cheesy knock-knock jokes,
a mascara stain on the shoulder of a tee-shirt,
shivers after a first touch,
"Thank yous" and "Hellos,"
fresh flowers woven in strands of braided hair,
anxious eyes gazing at the sun as it sets,
screams following the discovery of a bees nest,
a thumb slowly brushing one single tear
off a lonely, stress-ridden cheek,
nails shortened to stubs by crooked teeth,
drunken performances on the guitar where
fuzzy states allow for revelations,
dancing in the rain to the beat of the thunder,
kisses on foreheads with no reason or explanation,
a teddy bear so worn it's been re-sewn,
hands gripped so tightly as if afraid to part,
giggles after "I love yous," sobs after "goodbyes."

What's happy when it's raining

The sun, though it is not seen,
plants with their leaves turned up,
rocks with mossy tops,
gutters, umbrellas, raincoats,
grassy fields and desert plains,
dirt, lakes, rain boots, gardens,
rainbows and wishing wells,
the clouds, the wind,
the ocean and her creatures,
dogs whose fur coats
turn chocolate after running
in the back yard,
broken pianos, windows
left ajar, flickering lights,
the lonely bucket that dreams
for days of leaks in roofs,
empty backyard pools,
the angered thunder,
the irritated lightning,
and sorrowful,
unfortunate writers,

such as I.

velvet goodbyes

It's like waiting for the candle wax to melt
seemingly to its demise, dripping off
the glass slowly, like sweat, or tears,

It's like holding my breath underwater,
then realizing the water is hot,
ashy, skin melting lava,

It's like running a marathon and
finding that the heat of the sun
has evaporated all the water,

It's like finally catching your dream
after years of chasing and realizing
it's not all you thought it would be,

It's like standing naked in -10 degree
weather while it snows and the wind
bites at your now-purple skin,

It's like knowing you're about to fall
off a 500 foot ledge but losing the ability
to control your limbs, and voice,

It's like feeling that you have
so much more to do, more to give,
but not knowing how,

or where to start.

Her spirit drained from her face,
Her soul dripped from her eyelashes,
Her confidence shed from her skin,
all because he told her "she couldn't."

-women falling

velvet goodbyes

Her spirit rose from the ashes of their ignorance,
Her soul lit up like a gasoline-doused flame,
Her confidence radiated off her skin,
all because she told him "she could."

-women rising

113

As a clinically diagnosed
Perfectionist I have a
tendency to expect
order in everything.
Picture frames must be
parallel with windowpanes,
books neatly stacked in
alphabetical order by author,
oil paints arranged in
a perfect rainbow,
no grammatical errors in the
2AM coffee inspired essays,
nothing left unfinished, not a singl—

I could feel my heartbeat
I could hear it over my headphones
I touched my chest and
there it was,

I knew I was alive then

I knew I was alive then

I knew.

-tactile

I've been dreaming of white, lifeless walls
and what to fill them with.
Which hues of reds and purples
and blues to make such dull tapestries come to life.

I've been dreaming of snow, and how it covers
everything it touches, creating a whiteout.
A blank space. So colorless yet so beautiful.

I've been dreaming of a clean canvas
and a set of fresh paints.
Staring at the insides of my eyelids,

I've been dreaming about new beginnings.
Packing the bare minimum of clothes,
boarding a bus, and facing a new life
with courage, bravery, and maybe a little fear.
But a good kind of fear.
The kind of fear that is exciting.

I've been dreaming of car horns, street lights,
and busyness.

I've been dreaming of what it's like to
sit in a café and watch as people
bustle by in a hurry.
And I try to imagine
what their lives hold and how
different they are from mine.

velvet goodbyes

I've been dreaming
about apartments with brick walls,
coffee stains on tee shirts, the screech
of the subway as it approaches.

I've been dreaming of the opportunities
lurking in each building, the resources
around every corner.

I've been dreaming of the sun
setting behind a stretch of skyscrapers.

-blank canvas

emily curtis

III.

Guilt is not a feeling
that chains itself to
new beginnings.

You are a tragic masterpiece

A fatal delight.
Magnificent.
Catastrophic.

But you
don't want
to be put
on display
as they would
any other
piece of art,
no.

I wanted to kiss you last night.
It was New Year's Eve
and all I could think of
was if you had found yourself
another pair of lips
as the countdown began,
but my resolution was to
find someone who would
want to call me his,
and I'm not sure if you could ever do that.

-before the resolutions begin

Reasons why

When you stare into space
as if space was something you
would be able to see so clearly yet
you squint because you need glasses,
when your foot vibrates the floor
from bouncing your knees, a habit
you have yet to break that comes
when your mind is in dire need of things
to think of, when the sun
bounces off your hair and transforms
each strand into a soft velvet gold,
when you read and laugh and
I have no idea why you're laughing but
I laugh too because your smile makes me
happy, when your competitiveness
gets the best of you and you cross the line but
what they don't understand is you're just
passionate, and when you look at me with
that careless gaze.

Sometimes I find myself wishing
that my blessings were real people,
that I could shake their hands and
properly say "thank you,"

but then I remember that
some of them actually are.

-to those who love me relentlessly

Reflections from a teenage girl

Some of them have
soft hearts,
but hard shells.
It may take you a while
to crack them,
but you'll get there.

It's worth it.

Birds eye view

The shadows of the clouds,
the rough shape of the shoreline,
the maze of roads,
the patches of fields,
like puzzle pieces, here and there,
surrounded by houses, and
the ensemble of cars, like ants,
crawling around this way and that,
and the pools of water, oddly shaped,
but beautiful nonetheless,
it all was
so beautiful, you know.

He is in our music
He is in our food,
our homes,
and schools,
and stores,
and in how we love,
and in how we learn
to say hello.

-Culture

emily curtis

You're looking for
a voice to talk with
on the phone
when the roads
get boring
and I
am looking for
someone's sweater
to steal
when the snow
starts to settle.

You ask,
"why?"

I say,
"why not?"

I was wrong

Before I met you
I thought
my greatest love
would be
for the pen that
allowed these words
to fill these pages.

emily curtis

I like the word "tender"

It makes me think of
how I would imagine
your love to be.
Your touch. Tender.

When you move a
strand of hair behind
my ear. Tender.

When you say my name
so quietly you wonder if
I even heard it. Tender.

Holding your hand. Tender.
Saying goodnight. Tender.

And even—when it comes
to this—saying goodbye.

Tender.

velvet goodbyes

I imagine you kissing my fingertips.
You say,

"they are what make you you"

and I would laugh
because the thought
would scare me.

And you would smile
because you liked those fingertips.

Things that are blue that remind me of you

The beach, the waves,
sandy navy towels,
the blanket at the edge of my bed,
lips after kissing in the cold,
the shirt of a man passing by,
the sky because we're both beneath it,
the crinkled flower petals hidden
between pages of my favorite books that
in their younger, more vibrant days
formed a flower you gave me,
the rain when it pelts the lake,
my coffee mug, blueberry pie,
eyes—any pair—with a tint of hazel,
my pool floats, my sunglasses,
the nail polish I wore constantly
after you left, the walls of
my room, my tears,

my heart.

velvet goodbyes

This recipe is all wrong, I know it.
It will end in bitterness. Maybe
too much salt. But it's worth a shot.

-homemade love

You hide your eyes from the world
so they won't notice your vulnerability,
hang your head low, rest your hood over your forehead,
you know if they saw what I saw
all hell would break loose
and you would be exposed.

Don't worry, my love,
I see it all,
and I love it all.

-there's no need to hide that tender heart of yours

velvet goodbyes

I want to fall in love with you
the way a rain drop
drizzles
down a windowpane
after the pouring has stopped
and all is silent.

Slowly.

You wouldn't want the rain
to fall all at once, would you?

emily curtis

I wonder if you've ever
watched one of those
cheesy rom-com's where
in the end the two lovers
stop pretending
and run to each other
wholeheartedly.

I used to hate
those but,
I don't know, I just
wonder and think
and daydream and wonder and. . .

-would you ever run to me like that?

Kindness tells me
not to fret because
she only puts her
faith in certain people.

Why are you
so scared of
your own
emotions?

Do you think
they will reveal
too much?

Because honey,
your face has
more expression
than your words
ever will.

Spring

You loved me then
when the ground was soft
and the snow was melting
and our hearts were, too.

emily curtis

For the doctors who saved her life.

-I am thankful part 1

For the hair on her head that finally grew back.

-I am thankful part 2

She sneaks up on me
sometimes
when you're around.

-Awe

I've been with boys who have thought
they split my heart in two,

but they haven't.

I've known "friends" who whisper
half-truths
expecting me to crack,

but I won't.

I've lived through things I can't explain,
things I still don't understand,
things that should have killed me,

but they didn't.

God has had the power to destroy me
time and time again,

but He hasn't.

-and this is how I know I am strong

Those scars on my back,
they are not pretty,
but they are my only reminder
that I am lucky to hear my heartbeat at night
when it is quiet and the
soft humming of nothingness
is the only other thing I can hear.

And sometimes I forget that
when I wish them away.

-I know now they are more a part of me than anything else

velvet goodbyes

And this wound
is what makes me
who I am.

-I don't want it to leave

emily curtis

I rode in a plane once
and dreamt that I had
jumped out onto the
puffy pillowy clouds
but instead of going through them
I landed on them
and they were soft
and they were comforting
and I was safe

and all was good.

Felicity

I can only imagine
the tranquility of an
evening well spent
with a pen and notebook
in hand, sitting under
a willow tree, a soft
breeze playing with the
loose strands of my hair,
my dog by my side,
and my responsibilities,
stranded,
in a desert
somewhere
far
far away.

emily curtis

I was not meant
to stay in that town
I was not destined to only know
that small circle of people
whom I grew up with
I was designed to change
I was programmed to see new things
to explore
to create
to grow
to live.

velvet goodbyes

These walking cliché's
crowd the halls, making
it impossible for me
to get by.

They hold hands
and they kiss
and they say
sweet nothings
to each other
while I walk
hand in hand
with my independence,
                    even happier.

Only a memory

It's been a while, hasn't it?
It's been a while since we talked.
Remember when you used to
tell me I was prettier than
the morning sun and that
you loved me?
No?
Me either.
Maybe I am thinking of someone else.
I laugh.
Maybe, he says.
Maybe.

velvet goodbyes

Love is a forest
filled with ferns, and
evergreens, and
oaks that have been
withered by woodpeckers,
Love is a river,
a deep crystal blue
that shines when kissed by the sun,
Love is a Sunday morning
when worries are hidden
beneath the feathery pillows
where our heads rest,
Love is a full coffee mug,
the last page of a book,
a genuine apology,

Love is a soft whisper.

-Love is not a battlefield

What lived in simpler times

Coloring books brimming
with pages of rainbows
and poorly drawn horses,
dolls with curly brown
hair, the type of hair
I wished I had,
notebooks filled with
secrets and confessions,
left absentmindedly
on the tip of my bed
for anyone to reach—secrets
back then aren't like
secrets today—princess
costumes and karaoke
machines, saying
"I love you" to
anyone and everyone
and not knowing the depth
of my words, not knowing
the depth of my surroundings,
not knowing the depth of you.

velvet goodbyes

Don't you worry, my dear,
these faceless zombies
whose skulls are filled with dirt,
they won't mean anything to you
years from now.

Soon you will be free from
their bloody jaws.

And one day
I'll be living in Boston
walking down Boylston St.
with my headphones in
listening to some
catchy tune and I'll be
smiling because
I never let her
get under my skin,
and I never let him
catch me off guard,
and I never let you
drag me underwater with you
as you sank.

velvet goodbyes

I like these cobblestones,
I like these people,
they walk in different directions,
their heads down but they are all connected,
I like the sounds of the cars
fighting with each other,
I like the busy breaths
of the buildings, the sigh of the
fast food workers at around 9 o' clock,
I like how no one judges but also everyone judges,
and money is spent on items of clothing
that find their way to the backs of closets
because we all want to make an impression,
that's all we ever try to do,
and I like the history here,
it seems to be around every corner.

-the city

My brother is a replica of his grandfather,
stubborn, loud, silly, and independent,
so was another, my mother, but
she would never admit it, she cared
so much, almost too much, and
her husband, he was quiet, but
when he did speak, people listened,
one cousin studied law and
could easily outwit you in any debate,
another taught math to high-schoolers and
loved to fish, even in the cold,
and their father, he was tough as hell
and loved to tease but had a good heart,
his wife was even more good-hearted,
but lastly, the mother of us all,
survivor of cancer, sweetest human being
I have ever known, she loved every single one of us
unconditionally.

Just as I will love you.

-what I will tell my granddaughter when she asks about our
family

velvet goodbyes

I am from soup on Sunday's,
and the whistle of a tea kettle,
from the French Language
intertwined with the English,
from tiny rooms and worn brown rugs,
from mustard gas and PTSD,
I am from the quick shuffle of 52 cards,

I am from the word on the street,
from alternative music and Sunday school,
from stubbornness and sawdust,
four-wheeler rides, porch swings,
and nights of no sleep,

I am from hospital beds and
friendly nurses who remember my name,
from floppy sun hats and
sea glass, from the crackle of a fire,
from backyard treehouses and
self-made teepees hidden in the brush,
from tales of Christopher Robin and his friend Pooh,

I am from the snowy mountains,
from Zeb's and The Beggar's Pouch,
I am from the crisp breeze gusting against ski lifts,
from overly competitive board games
and The Office quotes,
from Thanksgiving Day pick-up football games.

I am from the number 10,
from wrapping paper,
from pet hair clinging to clothes,
from snow angels and hot chocolate,
from stained glass
and breaking bread.

Four years here
four years of my life
given to a town
I truly adore
and the people
and the laughter
and the food
and the traditions
and everything else
that comes with it
I wouldn't change a
thing and I wouldn't
give up any single memory
for the world,
each friendship
each heartache
and even each failure
was worth it
because
it shaped me into
this determined woman
the one that now sits here writing this
and now, as I leave,
I say thank you.

-velvet goodbyes

velvet goodbyes

About the Author

Emily Curtis is a poet based in a small Maine town.
Through her words she has blossomed into a confident
author of two self-published poetry collections. She enjoys
writing, reading Jane Austen novels, and drinking tea. Her
writing serves as an outlet, a way to share her story, as well
as the stories of others. She is currently attending
Emerson College in Boston, Massachusetts, where she
hopes to broaden her knowledge of literature and writing.
You can find her on Instagram as *@poetryflowssofter*.

www.ingramcontent.com/pod-product-compliance
Lightning Source LLC
Chambersburg PA
CBHW071856020426
42331CB00010B/2543